I0163598

AN ESSEX LAD

by

Mark Powell

Grosvenor House
Publishing Limited

All rights reserved
Copyright © Mark Powell, 2025

The right of Mark Powell to be identified as the author of this
work has been asserted in accordance with Section 78
of the Copyright, Designs and Patents Act 1988

The book cover is copyright to Mark Powell

This book is published by
Grosvenor House Publishing Ltd
Link House
140 The Broadway, Tolworth, Surrey, KT6 7HT.
www.grosvenorhousepublishing.co.uk

This book is sold subject to the conditions that it shall not, by way of
trade or otherwise, be lent, resold, hired out or otherwise circulated
without the author's or publisher's prior consent in any form of
binding or cover other than that in which it is published and
without a similar condition including this condition being
imposed on the subsequent purchaser.

A CIP record for this book
is available from the British Library

Paperback ISBN 978-1-83615-153-1
Hardback ISBN 978-1-83615-154-8
eBook ISBN 978-1-83615-155-5

"Art is not about understanding, it's about experience"
Antony Gormley

Omnibus Quos Amavimus

1

Generation to generation extending the line
Layer upon layer, to spawn is to share
Seed sows seed by innate design
New life created without fanfare.

All is begotten, nothing in isolation made
Bestowed or birthed, is anything unique or free?
Ocean breeds wave, forest the shade
To adore the apple is to love the tree.

2

Across the flatlands beacons burn
Suburb and shoreline gird and heed
At night our vulnerabilities return
To face the flame and then recede
For better tomorrow and Godspeed.

Daybreak rousing behind treeline
Soothing return of familiarity
An open hand we shouldn't decline
Though hand to clasp what we cannot see
The future is merely a memory.

South Weald sun splashes morning onto green
Rooted amid reveille's sound and heart
No trace of the haunting where night has been
With summer dawn's chiffon the ghosts depart
However, the past is always the start.

3

Wake: the stretching morning calls
On marshland tidal foam
Across sand flats and dockside walls
To the coastal cottage home.

Wake: the expectant morning calls
On concrete bridge over the tracks
Across the estate and spray-paint scrawl
To the paper boys and girls in cheap anoraks.

Wake: the rousing morning calls
The bus stop gathering its eight o'clock crowd
Off to all the various schools
Threatened under gathering cloud.

Wake: the stretching morning calls
Bacon sandwich and mug of sugared tea
Setting up the market stalls
Fruit and veg, shoes and jewellery.

Wake: the expectant morning calls
Team going to work on the stately home's lawns
Matching boots and overalls
"Mind the blades!" the head gardener warns.

Wake: the final morning calls
Forget the bus and down your drinks
Leave the stalls and down your tools
Cling for life and cry as the flatland sinks.

4

You were always a child of the damp
Comfortable crossing fields with mud-collecting boots
Familiar with slippery stiles and jutting tree roots
And the canvas tent of Boys' Brigade camp
Hymns and cocoa supper with captivating scent of the paraffin lamp.

You were always a child of the rain
Used to ashen skies that invariably drained onto the meadow walk
Sheltering under the hornbeam to wait and talk
Whilst admiring the crumpled, lush terrain
Aware we'd never stand beneath this tree again.

You were always a child of petrichor
Appreciating that it comes with the territory
Nature's postcoital tranquility
And the fading afternoon means therefore
We'll walk home in dusk's splendour.

5

Under the cloud the war memorial stands
Cut and chiselled into coloured bands
Saluting the sunset before shadows that seem
To smear their sadness across the village green.

Under charred sky the search for a clue
To bring us closer to the people we knew
Those who have gone and those who will soon
The footprints of heaven, the piper's last tune.

There are no stars over Blackmore tonight
Difficult to fathom the sterile blight
Eternal cosmos declines to confide
How big, how long, how deep, how wide.

6

Not of the country, not of the sea
Not of the city but of all three
Tiptree cottage to Heybridge mud
Romford bitter and Boudica blood
Hybrid land rather than ruptured twain
Of urban street and mud-stained lane
Meadow Rise and Warley Hill
Georgian farmhouse to tower block
Village cockneys and Romany stock
Potter Street, Netteswell and Burnt Mill
Suburban stage of eastern folk
Built upon the slaughtered oak.

And what kind of life is prepared for them?
For both the women and the men
The feasting or suffering that condemn
Which tortured loyalty cannot stem
Though this shall be a piece, a place, of home
Marked by signs or the Leper Stone
If not here and now, then where and when?
If not for forging tribe's delight
Then for whatever will come, despite
The endless hope of the prophet's pen
Viewed through fate's imperfect prism
The truth of Essex-stentialism.

ז

I heard a lad call out to me
As I was standing by the tree
He entered our garden through the gate
Assumed it was a boy from the council estate
Noticed he looked a lot like me
In shape and face, though a he not a she
His eyes were also a reflection of my own
Smiling handsomely outside my home.

He knew my name and seemed to suggest
That we were friends, "Oh, the best of the best."
But I'd never seen this boy before
So retreated politely towards the front door
I ran inside and crouched on the floor
Peered through the curtains but he was there no more
What did the boy want with me?
Then disappearing so inexplicably.

I saw him again from the bus to school
Standing by a hedgerow waving to us all
Drenched by rain he didn't seem to care
Still in the same clothes he obviously liked to wear
"Who knows that boy?" I asked, leaning over my seat
No one had seen the lad soaked from head to feet
Everywhere I went I expected him there
In a shop queue, in the park, at the visiting fair.

On my wedding day he was up in a tree
Joining the other guests throwing confetti
Though his was not made of paper or rice
But little stars with blazing shards, a gift from paradise
After giving birth to my first child
My biological mother and I reconciled
Adoption had proved the making of me
But I still craved completion for my own baby.

The woman sobbed for the years and the pain
If only the chance to go back again
She was young, poor, single and scared
Encouraged to give birth then surrender babies to care
"Babies?" I asked. "How can that be?"
I was the only child from the birth family
"Your brother died quickly, clinging to you
His eyes never opened, your hand all he knew."

And so I returned to the wedding day church
To see if my brother might appear on his perch
I called and I cried but he never did show
Gave up after three days with the first winter snow
I didn't see him again until
I was old, in a hospice, terminally ill
He looked through the window of the home
Still in those same clothes, still on his own.

On the day I died he was waiting for me
As the care staff mourned respectfully
I was at peace as I got up to go
Leaving my body to be buried below
My brother led me to a beautiful place
Where memory and age dissolved into space
We clung to each other at beginning and end
Oh the best of the best, my brother and friend.

8

Gilded Thames on the southern flank
Carrying the nation from core to shore
Coaxing the flow from gas-tank bank
To Southend Crowstone where it becomes river no more.

Not to deny the estuary dream
Water beckons and leads the way
Unity of river, creek and stream
Confirming allegiance to London clay.

Of lighterman, carman and stevedore
Twenty thousand strong plus ganger's delight
The burgeoning trade of the docks post-war
Cherished pilgrimage of cockney birthright.

Graft of a sinner, faith of a saint
Belonging is believing at sacrament's door
Hard and hobnailed, docker's penance restraint
Fuelled by inimitable esprit de corps.

9

To feel your closeness, breathe your air
Imagining a clandestine affair
What effect you have on me
In thrall to your radiance, your beauty
Hungering for the slightest touch
The merest look can mean so much
Sheer delight in dreams of you
Of a midnight hushed rendezvous
To yearn for even the briefest kiss
Anoint a precious love like this.

Such arousal in the allure
A desire so prurient yet so pure
Treasuring this carnal ache
Sensual splendour incarnate
Hanker to feel your hand in mine
Hoping to seed the embrace divine
No doubt or deed can dare constrain
Or spell of urging lust contain
To wonder what sorcery is cast on me
Ardour's wand wielded so powerfully.

10

The miasma drifts across Dagenham
Ford's late shift starts to arrive
Dirty air makes no difference to them
Cocooned in car to make the drive
From estate on the A13's north side.

Slowly the borough turns brown
Rotting sky is readying rain
Traffic clogged in and out of town
Closed lanes on the North Circular. Again
At least this summer we'll get down to Spain.

11

First love is the sweetest though often cursed
Under the dogwood tree walking arm in arm
Learning romance was extemporized, unrehearsed
Incipient emotions so susceptible to charm
Inevitable we became mutually immersed
Centre of each other's universe.

If just you and me then love would be easy
Without the world disrupting our joy
Yet autumn claims most every tree
Its frigid finger to deploy
But it was not solely nature's strategy
The venom of envy undid me.

The lecherous glare of every man
The secret lusts I swore you hid
Trysts with all my friends you planned
Our spring of love now flowed turbid
Unsure how this torment began
Yet jealousy filled and overran.

Your reassuring words and tearful pleas
Curtly rejected as ploys and lies
Deceit as some sadistic tease
Causing me to hate yet agonize
As to why you're begging me to be
The man I was under the dogwood tree.

12

Farewell to shed and shop and back door key
Farewell to the old Thames shore
And all those things that created me
For I come home no more.

Wandering alone on half-known roads
Collecting debris to store in the drawer
Mementos that time cruelly and unjustly corrodes
For I come home no more.

Caress my face and kiss my cheek
It is you whom I will always adore
The joyfulness has now turned bleak
For I come home no more.

We etched our names on the old school tree
Together forever whilst carving we swore
I was yours and you were mine unequivocally
Now I come back no more.

Can I embrace you one last time?
A moment's pause for love's encore
Heed the call to cross the line
I'm loath to leave and return no more.

The sweetest fruit has shortest life
Evades the harvest store
What was light is light no more
And now the closing door.

13

What becomes of me when I fall to final sleep?
Do I simply cease to be or go to a cursed or blessed eternity?
Perhaps a condition that's not so neat
Trapped in darkness ominously
Foredoomed under soil's own firmament
Conscious of my cramped predicament.

Alone with no sight or sound
Only thoughts to fill the space
The torturous vacuum of the ground
Wrapped in box and mud's embrace
What is this terrifying limbo state?
A phoney death conceived by fate.

Time to grieve not only for what has gone
But what remains forever apart
My home, my garden, my brother John
All I've known and now depart
The harrowing notion of life ongoing
While trapped below unseeing, unknowing.

To the ceaseless void I now belong
Fossilised yet continuing to think
Unimaginable enduring this torment for long
Is heart or mind the weakest link?
Confined by the cursed, physical castration
Doomed to the Eternal Separation.

14

Desolate patch of open land
Gallows Field at Gallows Corner
Scaffold shows direction and duty
Stained for criminal though sacred to mourner.

Many a neck submitted to rope
Body abandoned to iron cage or chains
The grisly marker for highway route
Potent exemplar the hangman ordains.

One hundred years of execution
Gradually faded from law
The final drop being two highwaymen
Then that was it, there were no more.

The relic weathered over time
Tormented frame resigned to rot
The many victims who had succumbed
Posterity erased and ultimately forgot.

Lord of the manor claimed the wood
Insisting on repurposed life
Still-strong lumber enough to construct
Two full-sized beds for squire and wife.

The carpenter went about his work
Despite an air of intolerance
From regular folk who seethed at thought
Of timber's ghoulish provenance.

Matching cots soon filled the room
As did the stench of death
The finest sheets and pillow spread
Failed to smother the gibbet's breath.

Candle extinguished on inaugural night
Darkness call for departed's ache
Lord and lady on eternal rafts
To sleep and never to wake.

15

Who can assuage this grief and help with the misery?
Why is there no mood thief to steal this sadness away from me?

Beware the hole bereavement's bored, tread carefully near the cavity
Avoid where emptiness is stored; life as it once used to be.

Dreams deceive with promises of what we fail to learn
Urge to remember and retrieve; but what has gone can never return.

16

Blood-orange glow in the Leather Bottle tonight
Regulars crowd into the public bar
Older cabal at table sitting upright
With cardigan, chain and unlit cigar
Nostalgic for happier times
When everybody knew their place and role
Sentimental about simpler crimes
When manors were so much easier to control.

What's become of things, they bemoan
No respect, no manners anymore
The clan had never felt so alone
Never been so easy to ignore
Most of the new breed were leaving the game
To be barrow boy, suit or self-employed instead
Not many using the family name
Even Ron's boy got a job and moved to Maidenhead.

17

Cans of Special Brew resting on cemetery stones
Hot knifing cannabis listening to cassettes
Dancing on ancestral bones
Before fading into our own silhouettes.

Within the year three of us were gone
One in a car crash, one in a fight
The last took pills (she said she wouldn't live long)
Trio of funerals held in candlelight.

It wasn't the future we had planned
To live in parallel, age side by side
The bitter truth of carpe diem's hand
The grasp at life can be denied.

Once a year we stand by the graves
Sipping beers to remember them
A toast to the past and future raves
The one-word epitaphs: *Resurgam.*

18

Morning smile with left eye swollen shut
But it was strained, the face complained, bottom lip also cut
Not unusual for the lad to arrive bruised
Stares from fellow pupils acknowledged and excused
Once a bicycle crash, another time a fall
Later, on crutches hobbling to school
Accident-prone they'd say with each hospital stay
After the ambulance had taken him away.

New head started at the beginning of academic year
Waited at school gate for the students to appear
Often noticed the boy's face and halting walk
Invited him to his office to have "a little talk"
The boy was reluctant to offer any clues
As to reasons for the limp and unsightly bruise
"Please understand that you are not to blame
No reason to be embarrassed, no need to be ashamed."
Within a week he'd moved to his aunt's house in Grays
Chose not to return home, even in the holidays.

Twenty years later near Maylandsea
Renovating a steeple with his specialist carpentry team
The vicar's face was familiar but now masked by a beard
From teacher now to preacher the recognition appeared
"How are you, sir? I'm an old pupil from school."
The briefest squint, a subtle stare, before the stunned recall
Impossible to forget the face of that child
"How wonderful to see you," the former teacher smiled
They share histories of the lives they have led
Genuine sense of kinship between the former boy and head
The men clasp hands with the unspoken background they both knew
The boy looks straight into the eyes, "You saved my life. Thank you."

19

My heart waits, my heart waits
For the cuckoo moon
It's when she promised she'd be back
And, my darling, not a moment too soon.

My heart waits as the days and weeks drift
Towards the cuckoo moon
When what will be the sweetest gift
Breathed scent of your perfume.

My heart is full, can barely wait
Tomorrow is the day
The cuckoo moon is here at last
My love is on her way.

My heart waits under the cuckoo moon
For the moment of return
The constant thoughts I've had of you
Your love for which I yearn.

Dawn has spilled its open wound
All night I stood in place
Unmoved beneath the cuckoo moon
It retreats now into space.

Don't fear, my love, for I'll remain
Until you can appear
Firm and steadfast here I am
I will wait another year.

20

He stored his self on the uppermost shelf
She buried her heart in a wooded part
He stashed his hope in the hollow of a tree
She hid her soul in a hole
He locked his spirit and swallowed the key.

21

On the Monday after Twelfth Night
The farming year begins
Ploughed dolly wards off harvest blight
Absolution for agrarian sins.

The lads arrive from Red Rose Farm
Pulling plough from home to home
Collecting coin through threat of harm
For seeds of shame that can't be sown.

On the market square in pearls
To Molly dance the day
Girls as boys and boys as girls
The vicar head to foot in hay.

For on this date the future's planned
A bid to fortune sway
Deter a curse upon the land
The hope of Plough Monday.

22

I held your hand on Hay Green Lane
Summer-bloomed love was but the start
Infatuation was hard to restrain
Cherishing fate-met counterpart
Yes, I learnt it all by heart.

I held your hand on altar's day
The pride of the village, the queen of brides
Although the weather was wet and grey
The brightest light from spirit guides
Yes, the spoil of love equally divides.

I held your hand as you ebbed away
At least you were at home and in your bed
In the profoundest silence I tried to convey
Something of love with your journey ahead
Yes, I wish it was me instead.

23

Looking across Clacton's shore
To the beach where we used to play before
We grew old like the pier limping into the sea
Into time, with Mum, Dad and the family.

The steel frame rusting from exposure
Losing its dignity and structural composure
The anglers leaning against the rails
Braving North Sea rain and south-easterly gales.

Ham and mustard sandwich eaten under duffel coat hood
Rarely has a packed lunch tasted so good
Pursuing moments from the past
The expectant chase with each bite, each cast.

But the incoming wave does not repeat
There's no resurrection mere valiant retreat
The ferocity of the coastal onslaught
Resolves with froth and a dying thought.

24

What can be built on Chelmer's bank?
With honour as foundation stone
A citadel to inspire and bolster rank
For those who call the county home:
The cabbie, the cook, the lad in the hat
The plumber, the postie, the aristocrat.

Sworn oath sealed with cutting blade
To secure our own Elysian Field
Sisters and brothers rise from the grave
With Trinovantes' jewels and war-blooded shield
For the heroes who rallied and fought for the cause
Proud to be outcasts, Britain's outlaws.

25

I promise to be gentle
Soft as the midnight breeze
Tender as the summer stream
Reassuring as the trees.

26

I open the book to the page of my life
To read it once more and re-read it again
Does it have clues to the inimitable rite
That teaches Essex boys to become Essex men?
Icons of Barking and Dagenham stay
Holding the torches as beacons are lit
Burning for Maldon, Burnham, Thorpe Bay
Bobby Moore and Alf Ramsey in Three Lions kit
It's what we've been told since babes in the pram
The ways of the world and rules of the game
How all the greatest legends began
Earning their stripes before wider acclaim.

27

Slender is the love that binds
Seeming too delicate to withstand
But if our affections remain aligned
There's hope to live the way we planned.

Times where doubt feeds into fear
Raging sea upon the rocks
Forgiveness will always draw us near
To soften blows and take the knocks.

But to overcome is to find your voice
Rise above the cynic's sneer
How you feel is merely choice
To frown or smile or scoff at fear.

28

The boys from Nine Ashes and the lads from the church
The girls from Stondon, Hook End and Spriggs
Young people no longer but alive in the birch
Reincarnated as leaves, branches and twigs.

Mothers and fathers call for their kids
Searching for those that nature stole
Marathon quest as sleeping forbids
Hope of recovery for the shire's fresh souls.

Who is redeemed when dark turns to light?
And still there remains the deserted bed
Be warned of wailing all day and all night
There's no consolation, the children are dead.

29

At the wedding reception you sat beside me
I was a cousin of the bride, you a friend of the family
Impeccably neat with soft-set hair
Delicate but regal on the black velvet chair
Chatted politely over meal with white wine
A nod, a smile, and the subtlest sign
Of mutual attraction perceived by sixth sense
Dismissing the significant age difference
Fifty years younger, a generation between
But passion is footloose and rebellious it seems
Tried to compose and desire assuage
Turned attention to the cover band taking the stage
Mingled and danced when the music began
Observed you later chatting with Nan.

Not one breath of sleep as thinking of you
Debating if and how to pursue
I phoned a week later, suggested coffee
"To see you again, it would be so lovely."
"I'm not sure it's wise," she said with regret
"I don't want to cause any family upset."
I promised discretion, "Between you and me?"
Agreed on next Thursday, eleven-thirty
Arrived at her house nervous then blushed
At sight of her fitted dress and thinning hair brushed
We talked about the wedding, my work, her love of ballet
Ogled her slyly when she brought in the tray
Avoided my gaze as she poured out the teas
Widowed ten years and her daughter overseas.

The fourth time I visited we kissed in the hall
As I was leaving, by the coats on the wall
"You silly thing. An old woman like me?"
But we kissed again, though delicately
Mottled hands grasping mine as if to say
I think you should go but I want you to stay
Such silence in the house that afternoon
Ascended the stairs to the guest bedroom
Loving undress and caring caress
Of tissue-like skin and small, wilted breasts
The joy of being gentle with the softest of sighs
Your fragile limbs and watery eyes.

30

Hate's habitat is found among the debris and holes
Amid the players and layers of failed goals
Defeat and envy seep into the smallest rift
Rupturing kinship and cutting kindness adrift.

What can be given from woman to man
from man to woman from prayer to plan?
Knowing acceptance of all that can go wrong
Fear for the feeble, an omen for the strong.

But peril is imminent for those who chose
To foment resentment and chop the rose
There is no mercy for those who seek
To better themselves at the expense of the weak.

31

The final words before dying that night
"Look, it's my brother, Paul, and Jimmy from school."
Eyes briefly bright in hospital light
"They're here to meet me. Oh, I've missed them all."

The dead, they say, welcome their own
When time has come to make the call
Not with sceptre, bouquet or throne
But with memory alone.

32

The hope in recovering what is lost
Is never free but comes with cost
And what is lost is sometimes found
In memory, feeling, sight and sound.

The things she hoped for, the things she'd done
Her things of beauty, her things of fun.
The eulogy of a child much loved
Now lowered into graveyard mud.

Trying to fathom what life has become
There were two daughters now just one
Plagued by thoughts of time before
Hysterical on the kitchen floor.

But something in the home's amiss
Experiences that cannot be dismissed
Feel the chill in the upstairs air
Hear the footstep on the stair.

The scent of her perfume drifts through the hall
Her mobile number in midnight call
A random cough, sometimes a sigh
"Are you there, my darling, did you not die?"

The hope in recovering what is lost
Is never free but comes with cost
And what is lost is sometimes found
In memory, feeling, sight and sound.

33

Blackwater ebbs and flows with the mud
Bringing the surge of ancestral blood.

Rotting hulks and rowboats lie aground
Dishevelled and limp, hollow and drowned.

The sludge is stoic until the tide weeps
Secured by current the debris sweeps.

Along the channel to the marshland shore
Where the local lads fished but fish no more.

34

Sullen the man who drinks alone
Fomenting gloom in the pub home from home
All become anxious when shadows approach
To load the luggage on Reaper's coach.

But behold the soul in the Gardeners Arms
Languishing as a pint of pale ale calms
Quiet man drinking in corner-seat shade
Countenance corrupted but never betrayed.

It was not the life he expected it to be
As a boy growing up in Tilbury
The promise of docks and waterside trade
Gave way to war and military parade.

One hundred hours before joining the fight
Into sky that adrenaline bleached white
Went down twice, the first time at sea
Plucked from waves for week's recovery.

Second time as a more seasoned flier
Bailed from the cockpit with both legs on fire
Over Leigh-on-Sea the chute deployed
Rooftop and railings managed to avoid.

The burnt limbs took a long time to heal
Right-side flesh remained crimped orange peel
The blaze thankfully avoided the face
Medals upstairs in an old pillowcase.

Yet no one knows when he's sat on the bus
Or when the neighbours are making a fuss
About parking and prices and the noise of the train
He's just a grandad who walks with a cane.

And so to that drink in the Gardeners Arms
Content with alcohol's companionable charms
Herald the heroes who sit there alone
The brave, the fearless, the hallowed unknown.

35

Mother left when he was three
Blamed himself for not being loveable
Fought the sadness, the misery
Those lost days gone, unrecoverable.

And now the bond of dad and daughter
In delight of the adored
Rebuilds the trust on familial altar
Where love is now at last assured.

36

Apologies for my eczema skin
The scaly red rash from cheek down to chin
Desperately wish I could change the view
To a complexion more agreeable to you.

Precise words and phrases anchored in memory
Recall exact moment when words said to me
That punctured the spirit and deflated the heart
"Crater Face," "Titch," "I thought you were smart."

Leaning against the youth club wall while the cool couples kissed
Unnoticed silhouette of shy hedonist
If only to be all the things in my head
Reluctantly resigned to reverie instead.

37

Who's to shuffle and mark the last cards?
And explain the meaning of who we were
On buttercupped grass of calm churchyards
It's silence that the dead prefer.

Are there clues in the final word?
A revelation from the brink
The whispered message unnoticed, unheard
Perhaps a key, the missing link.

Who's the one to direct the way?
Along the hamlet's foggy lane
Or guide the ship to sheltered bay
Where voyage will wait until safe again.

Be it the cross, star or crescent you chase
Or pagan rites in which you believe
For sorrow tomorrow will take its place
Eternal contemplation is yours to receive.

38

On daybreak duvet draped in pain
From drunken night carousal with amphetamine support
To swear you'll never do it again
Soberly promised yet coming to nought
There's agony in the wasted awake
All day to suffer the dread and headache
Pity me, old sport.

Wince at half-remembered things
What did we do, what did I say?
Muffle the phone with its terrifying rings
Stench of booze and spilt ashtray
Partying obscene till comatose
Coming round in bloodied clothes
Pity me, I pray.

39

Farewell, young tyke, does your mother know
That you are leaving home?
Taking the train on the District line
To explore the world alone.

The streets will make a man of you
If you learn from proper friends
Though maybe it will make a meal or two
Feasting on young blood's dividends.

The empty bedroom left to wait
For son's return; where it all began
But will that young boy ever come back?
For sure he'll be a man.

40

The ancient wood's in trouble, it can sense the impending axe
Trunks and branches readying for coordinated attacks
The lumbermen chat and idle, preparing to destroy
Nature betrayed by sharpened blade, look away sweet girl and boy.

To witness war upon our land is not to death condone
As long as concrete dissolves to dust the land will claim its own
Is this progress for our time, to build and strive and grow?
Can the slave for freedom plot and master overthrow?

Confined within the furrowed life made for us by the plough
To climb the rut and seek beyond the rules will not allow
Bankers and brokers on the train, the plumber in her van
The shop assistant rides the bus, the architect with his plan.

But Smiler lives within the wood under homemade canopy
His pots and pans and open fire define simplicity
Every day is lived anew with nothing to constrain
Each moment a gold link added on, such beauty in the chain.

Life is light with little owned, no kingdom to sustain
Shed the heavy cloak of stuff to freely breathe again
Very few encroach upon Smiler's woodland camp
They see the tent and smell the smoke, bypass the bearded tramp.

Tremendous joy in being alone, no social duty weighs
The chance to be at liberty from other souls' malaise
But if it's true you only become you through interaction with others
Then we must wonder who is this man without sisters or brothers?

He lives with trees and even these now let out an anxious moan
The trembling leaves reveal the fear of imminent dethrone
Smiler awaits the lumberjacks, he can hear them at the rim
The initial chop makes him drop, wretched from limb to limb.

Smiler dies on nature's ground to fade into the moss
The axe chop sounds the darkest knell for man and forest's loss
Thus, if it's true you only become you through interaction with others
Wonder again who is this man dying without sisters and brothers?

41

Marvel the contours of the dress
Shaped splendour in the hip and breast
Delicate fabric guides desire's eyes
Lustful throes I can't disguise
Adoring the softness and maturity
Overwhelmed by your irresistibility
Blushing, nervous, in proximity
Thoughts of tenderest intimacy
The whispered, "Please be gentle," that I pine for
Frock sliding to the bedroom floor.

Every night I think of you
I know I shouldn't but I do
For there can be no consummation
Mere wondrous release in imagination
As sadly this love can never be
Consigned to romantic reverie
Accepting this love must be constrained
The desperate longing disciplined, contained
Its cherished fervour unrevealed
Rapture's lips forever sealed
So many words will be left unsaid
So many poems left unread.

42

From morning's yawn, the first sunshine
On Ongar at the end of the Central line
Slouching down the approach again
Schoolday routine of underground train.

Skinheads with leaflets outside the station
Peddling notion of Anglo-Saxon nation
White laces for British Movement, red for National Front
Beseeching the bespectacled grammar school runt.

Carriages fill with uniformed horde
Students from six different schools on board
Smoking carriages host the in-crowd
Under honeycomb-coloured ceiling and tobacco cloud.

Theydon Bois, Loughton, Buckhurst Hill
Woodford, South Woodford, Snaresbrook until
Stop by stop the pupils leave
Ongoing commuters breathe relieved.

Disembark at Debden with the Davenant boys
Glad for air and respite from noise
No rush for assembly so sit with a friend
On wooden bench at platform's end.

The seat affords a perfect view
Of passengers waiting on Platform Two
A couple of schoolboys killing time
As train approaches on the opposite line.

Woman in blue raincoat stands aloof
Just beyond the station roof
Scant indication of any fear to hide
With Sainsbury's shopping bag clutched by her side.

She throws herself under the train's front wheels
Pushed along by her shoulders and heels
Rag-doll head repeatedly smashing the track
Mangled body wrapped in charred and shredded mac.

We study the mess then flee the scene
Safety from horror by the chocolate vending machine
The woman chose to die on the Central line
Tuesday morning, just before nine.

43

To die in the flames, the martyred divine
The melting of flesh and inferno of hair
William Hunter stood true to belief
Commitment to cause that beckoned grief
Communion invite did stoutly decline
Cremated with grace in contemplative prayer.

This sacrificial pyre directed the way
Fervour and faith flow thick in our veins
Delight in the dust of Hunter's remains
For commitment to cause is freedom from chains
The fire that burned that early March day
Still blazes away and forever sustains.

44

There's commotion at the travellers' site
Set half a mile from town
Cars and trucks arriving tonight
For new champion to crown.

Scattered herd of caravans
Fence the secretive tribe
Rituals gathered as well as plans
With oral tradition life's inscribed.

Born and bred for honoured brawl
Bare-knuckles the stuff of home
Though never for glory or for spoil
Simply to represent their own.

Many fists are shredded to bone
From hours spent slugging the bag
Footwork honed by evenings alone
Then about the ring for sparring tag.

Warriors robed in hessian sacks
Warm up with pals on pads
Encouraging slaps greet the backs
To circle of hay bales and jeering lads.

When fight is done there's nothing lost
But pride that they had stood
The blood and broken nose small cost
To become the men they knew they could.

45

Raised overhead for all to see
Preventing our downfall, evading the abyss
And seeing off calamity
No reason to recall, no need to reminisce
For nothing can befall these lands
So long as the Kelvedon Hatch transmitter stands.

And what is built above us
Radiates beyond
Doubts and opposition treasonous
The wrong way to respond
For the presaging of golden days
So long as the skeletal structure stays.

What belongs to the future is invariably the past
As we wait and wait for passing time
Better to be ready, remain steadfast
To accept the paradigm
And hope to hope the radio mast
Will endure and will outlast.

If hourglass measures falling sand
And sundial marks the rays
Then as the steel-built sky is spanned
It surveys the cultural waves
There to know such fitting power
The flatland's very own Eiffel Tower.

46

"Don't get old before your time,"
Said a wise old lady
But I was underage and wanted a drink
So her words were no use to me.

"The difference between love and lust,"
Explained when I was young:
"When the deed is done
Do you want to stay or do you want to run?"

"Always be yourself."
The well-worn coin of advice
But I'm a fool and quite ill-bred
Much better to pretend to be somebody nice.

47

You never mentioned that you were desperately sad
Even when twenty and lost your dad
Perhaps the misery explains the hedonism
Rather than youthful exuberance or the stint in prison.

Only later came hints of the strain
Drunken ramblings and allusions to pain
Had no idea you were so unhappy inside
Didn't know what to say the first time you cried.

Year after year of self-medication
Then the overdose at Colchester station
Few weeks recovering in hospital ward
A chance to get your spirit restored.

On discharge you planned a new beginning
Work was picking up and Arsenal started winning
But beneath the facade something was wrong
Despite the brave face you didn't have long.

Reinforced the bedroom joists with struts of four-by-two
Ensuring it had the strength to take the weight of you
Anticipating the moment, the fateful triggered time
To surrender yourself to sleep and silence traitored mind.

Door remained unanswered and phone to voicemail
Curtains permanently closed and your car no longer for sale
What did you think when you stood on the chair
Put your head through the rope and steadied yourself there?

What did you think when you stepped from the perch
For the ceiling to heave and your whole body lurch?
Was it a moment of joy or despair
When the noose pulled tight and you pedalled the air?

48

Here is the recollection shared between friends
The knowing smile of experiences past
Nostalgia attempts to make amends
The flag of memory at eternal half-mast.

Here is the memory put into frame
The bride looks happy but the groom looks rough
One thousand to choose from yet all look the same
Sometimes one photograph is more than enough.

Here is the memory put into words
Articulated by definition, context and codes
In hope that the writer to reader confers
Something of meaning in life's episodes.

49

Summer job at the county library
Schooldays done for this lad of the shire
Familiar face assigned to induct me
A man from church who sings in the choir.

Gentle, well-spoken, though eccentric in style
In mottled tweed suit, pocket hankie dandified
We live close-by; no more than half a mile
"I'm going your way, old chap. Let me give you a ride."

He lives alone in a cottage overlooking the pond
Orderly garden with apple and plum trees
Boys snigger rumours but I do not respond
This charming man has no duty to please.

Shared drive to work inspires me awake
Chatty return followed by daily invite:
"Why don't you come in for some tea and cake?"
I decline politely then ponder all night.

I'm no ladies' man and yet to be kissed
A late developer, barely in bloom
Yet inchoate stirring of passions I've missed
Explored alone in midnight bedroom.

Right or wrong to embrace the ache
For glorious submission to covert delight
"Why don't you come in for some tea and cake?"
I decline once again but with internal fight.

Sunday at church he's there in the choir
My face throbbing red with a secret so near
White surplice and purple cassock, such draped desire
The modesty of lust is merely veneer.

Our eyes connect from nave to stall
Hymn book unstable in trembling grip
Body alight with enraptured enthral
What has become of this library friendship?

A tense silence on Monday's journey home
Restrained conversation, though awkwardly we tried
What imagination has conjured and repeatedly shown
Can struggle to appear before reality's eyes.

Eager to give and desperate to take
Village approach for the familiar line:
"Why don't you come in for some tea and cake?"
"Yes, I will," I say, because now is the time.

50

I look over my shoulder to wave Trevor away
That's how I remember it, or at least that's what I say
It was only the second day back at school
After the summer break
It was therefore an easy mistake to make.

It was certainly chaotic outside the gate
Where the parents and guardians stood to wait
For the charge of boys, girls, bags and bikes
At half past three
To be back home in time for telly and tea.

He pushed on the pedals and pulled back on the handlebars
To wheelie through a gap in the idling cars
But a driver on the wrong side of the road
Going too fast
Turned best mate Trevor from the present into the past.

51

The Leather Bottle was always busy in the public bar
Full of it with banter, bravado and casual violence
But for days after Dave's son, Trevor, got killed by the car
The pub, to a man, sat there in silence.

52

No finer sight than the furnished elm
On woodland path or pastoral scene
The erupting branches overwhelm
The memorial bench on Horsefayre Green
Herald the crowning of this year's May Queen.

By the water's edge the willow weeps
Sobbing in ripples that pattern the pond
Just for this moment recollection sleeps
And the city, suburb and town respond
To the villagers' unique, unbreakable bond.

So rich and light the small-leaved lime
Shimmering fragrance of forest's past
The longing for another life, another time
Though nature never stops to ask
Can this beauty be surpassed?

The august but eccentric silver birch
Of royal stock yet refusing to laud
With armoured honour from elegant perch
Thrust into soil as Templar's sword
Soil's prime spot is just reward.

Such pride in a line of London planes
Dictatorial and certain of their cause
Viewed at distance from Lovers Lane
Hand in hand the sweethearts pause
As the evening light withdraws.

53

Hear the battle cry
Under dismal Havering sky
Amid the stench of brewery
Harsh sweetness but also bitter, herby.

Gangs gather on the market square
Organized inter-town warfare
Troops from Brentwood, Harold Wood, Gidea Park, Laindon
Upminster, Ilford, Tilbury and Rainham.

Golf clubs, knives and studded bats
Knuckledusters secured under hand wraps
Brotherhood of the hometown mate
Enemies by the precinct congregate.

What awaits in combat is not given a thought
Pumped for our own generation's Agincourt
Neighbourhood armies set to collide
Attack together, side by side.

Battles evolve into scattered zones
Casualties falling to the cobblestones
One boy lies crumpled, comatose
Bleeding from his mouth, ears and nose.

Police units arrive leaping from white vans
The fighting stops and troops disband
With warriors having abandoned the scene
The boy's dead body is draped in blue polythene.

54

The pebbledashed houses along the main road
Facade the feelings
And thoughts about themselves
Few can pay for what they owe
Holiday souvenirs
On living room shelves.

Hindsight thrives in unhappy soil
Roots tangled and tormented
Beneath adjacent cul-de-sac
The one-way street inside us all
No return, no replay
No turning back.

55

The yen to return to childhood home
The family days of Mum and Dad
Nestling politely on Ingatestone Road
Brief moments were, ultimately, all that we had.

Strange to travel from boy to middle-age
Pathway of time hardly noticed barely laid
Recollection and nostalgia can never assuage
Locked doors of the past memory betrayed.

What chance for us here, stuck in the now?
Any cure for bereavement, what remedy?
Ready for regrowth with the turn of the plough
Churning life's soil, sowing seeds of me.

56

The county can kill but the country can cure
Harvesting life from damp copse and moor
The saffron crocus is a wondrous thing
Bounty of October when gathered in
Orange stigma in lush purple gown
Dried over fire till horse chestnut brown
Add ransoms to this concoction of health
To bring healing, good feeling, wisdom and wealth
As the Maldon flats bestow the sweetest samphire
Twined handfuls sold to ruddy-cheeked buyer.

Hail Dido's apothecary
In Hainault Forest set under tree
An elixir composed to succour the soul
Revive the spirit and anguish console
Famed ointment of fresh green fern
Cooked by cauldron then poured into urn
Dispensed on Thursdays and sworn by all
Potion's power in medicinal enthral
The promise to share the vaunted recipe
Vowed in vain when Dido died unexpectedly.

57

The sun at noon urges playful delight
Hot air harmony to squint in light
Stripped down for summer in bare chests and tats
Barbecue and sound system outside the flats.

Torched flesh lying on open-space green
Blankets and towels spread out in between
Five-a-side football and Frisbee throws
Doors and windows wide open at the old folks' bungalows.

Boys on benches by the parade of shops
Smoking and spitting wearing vests and flip-flops
Little lads one-handed on bikes clutching ice-cream
Bikini girls splashing in tree-canopied stream.

Eternal evening before the briefest of night
Elevates car race and drunken pub fight
Sweat-drenched bed is small price to pay
For suburban glory on the year's hottest day.

58

What do I see when I look at the sun's flight?
A brightness in the mind
Beyond the mundane of secular invite
To succour the spirit, a feeling aligned.

In the afternoon sky of faded denim blue
With cuts and slashes of angular white
Manhandled to the horizon as evening's mildew
Spreads its stain over day's dying light.

But darkness the harbinger of other truths
Passing, transition, closure, peace
Smothering like smoke the village roofs
No heavenly glow to offer release.

59

What can be said of such a love
With moments measured in tears
The passion was never going to be enough
To lessen the suffering and other people's sneers.

Penitent words and the promise to change
Renew and pledge to the idyll
Refusing to succumb to the fated estrange
It's in our own hands, just a matter of will.

How many loves are worth fighting for?
Each naive yet knowing in their own way
Such are the vagaries of the sliding door
Hoping it will slide no more.

60

On top of broad shoulders bolstered by pride
Cheering we carried you from victory's field
Elated, not one of us remained dry-eyed
What dreams had promised our brotherhood sealed.

And now six months later we carry you aloft again
On top of our shoulders weakened with grief
From the church out into the graveyard rain
Drenched under coffin, tears of disbelief.

61

Our love was never meant to be
A road untravelled imposed on me
Passion chained by circumstance
Dreams alone served the romance.

Furtive desire sustained alone
Fantasies condemned to the unknown
Despite the desperate yearning for you
All too soon the hope was through.

Watching the longing go up in smoke
Sitting solemnly as the vicar spoke
At the Bentley Crematorium on the A128
Your eulogised life to celebrate.

Adored in secret all those years
Little surprise there were no tears
Accustomed to absence and the loss
The burden of infatuation's albatross.

Despite mute ardour's easy disdain
It inflicts its own particular pain
A failed romance is gallant but not the same
As the love which dies unloved, unclaimed.

62

There are no stars over Blackmore tonight
Molasses sky spread from tragedy hewn
Urging forgiveness to banish the blight
Not a single star here, not even a moon.

The village green of childhood games
Now lies fallow, overgrown
I can see the faces, hear the names
But youth's no more, I stand alone.

In the damp soil away from it all
Don't spare the spade please bury me deep
Muffle the hymns of the funeral
Between loam and lid long shall I sleep.

63

It's time to walk on Wenlocks Lane
From road to footpath then bridle trail
The summer heat hazes the rural plain
Blanching the towering poplars pale.

Across the field towards the church
Steeple a watchtower for county reign
Deign the noble cross at perch
Girded by stoic weather vane.

Accept decorum as one should
By the daffodils propped atop a mound
Manicured grass where the vicar stood
Interring souls in sacred ground.

July's fragrance speaks lovingly
Of what the years have made
A grave in the corner by the tree
Bejewelled by dappled leafy shade.

Where you stand, friend, so did I
With nonchalant grace, no price to pay
And little thought that I would die
But there I was, now here I lie.

www.ingramcontent.com/pod-product-compliance
Lightning Source LLC
Chambersburg PA
CBHW021939040426
42448CB00008B/1146